SNAPSHOTS OF A
DAUGHTER-IN-LAW

SNAPSHOTS OF A DAUGHTER-IN-LAW

◈

POEMS

◈

1954-1962

◈

Adrienne Rich

W · W · NORTON & COMPANY · INC ·

NEW YORK

Some of the poems in this book first appeared in *The Beloit Poetry Journal, The Critical Quarterly* (Great Britain), *Harper's Magazine, The Nation, Paris Review, Partisan Review, Poems in Folio, Portfolio and Art News Annual, New Poets of England and America No. 2,* and *Penguin Anthology of Modern American Poetry.* "At Majority" and "From Morning-Glory to Petersburg" appeared originally in *The New Yorker.* "Readings of History" was presented as the 1960 Phi Beta Kappa poem at the College of William and Mary.

CONTENTS

A JOHN SIMON GUGGENHEIM MEMORIAL FELLOWSHIP
AND AN AMY LOWELL TRAVELLING SCHOLARSHIP BOTH
CONTRIBUTED GREATLY TO THE YEARS DURING WHICH
MUCH OF THIS BOOK WAS WRITTEN.

SNAPSHOTS OF A
DAUGHTER-IN-LAW

◈ AT MAJORITY
— for C. —

When you are old and beautiful,
And things most difficult are done,
There will be few who can recall
Your face that I see ravaged now
By youth and its oppressive work.

Your look will hold their wondering looks
Grave as Cordelia's at the last,
Neither with rancor at the past
Nor to upbraid the coming time.
For you will be at peace with time.

But now, a daily warfare takes
Its toll of tenderness in you,
And you must live like captains who
Wait out the hour before the charge—
Fearful, and yet impatient too.

Yet someday this will have an end,
All choices made or choice resigned,
And in your face the literal eye
Trace little of your history,
Nor ever piece the tale entire

Of villages that had to burn
And playgrounds of the will destroyed
Before you could be safe from time
And gather in your brow and air
The stillness of antiquity.

1954

◈ FROM MORNING-GLORY TO PETERSBURG
(The World Book, 1928)

"Organized knowledge in story and picture"
    confronts through dusty glass
    an eye grown dubious.
I can recall when knowledge still was pure,
    not contradictory, pleasurable
    as cutting out a paper doll.
You opened up a book and there it was:
    everything just as promised, from
    Kurdistan to Mormons, Gum
Arabic to Kumquat, neither more nor less.
    Facts could be kept separate
    by a convention; that was what
made childhood possible. Now knowledge finds me out;
    in all its risible untidiness
    it traces me to each address,
dragging in things I never thought about.
    I don't invite what facts can be
    held at arm's length; a family
of jeering irresponsibles always
    comes along gypsy-style
    and there you have them all
forever on your hands. It never pays.
    If I could still extrapolate
    the morning-glory on the gate
from Petersburg in history—but it's too late.

1954

RURAL REFLECTIONS

This is the grass your feet are planted on.
You paint it orange or you sing it green,
    But you have never found
A way to make the grass mean what you mean.

A cloud can be whatever you intend:
Ostrich or leaning tower or staring eye.
    But you have never found
A cloud sufficient to express the sky.

Get out there with your splendid expertise;
Raymond who cuts the meadow does no less.
    Inhuman nature says:
Inhuman patience is the true success.

Human impatience trips you as you run;
    Stand still and you must lie.
It is the grass that cuts the mower down;
It is the cloud that swallows up the sky.

1956

THE KNIGHT

A knight rides into the noon,
and his helmet points to the sun,
and a thousand splintered suns
are the gaiety of his mail.
The soles of his feet glitter
and his palms flash in reply,
and under his crackling banner
he rides like a ship in sail.

A knight rides into the noon,
and only his eye is living,
a lump of bitter jelly
set in a metal mask,
betraying rags and tatters
that cling to the flesh beneath
and wear his nerves to ribbons
under the radiant casque.

Who will unhorse this rider
and free him from between
the walls of iron, the emblems
crushing his chest with their weight?
Will they defeat him gently,
or leave him hurled on the green,
his rags and wounds still hidden
under the great breastplate?

1957

◈ THE LOSER

A man thinks of the woman he once loved:
first, after her wedding, and then nearly a
decade later.

1

I kissed you, bride and lost, and went
home from that bourgeois sacrament,
your cheek still tasting cold upon
my lips that gave you benison
with all the swagger that they knew—
as losers somehow learn to do.

Your wedding made my eyes ache; soon
the world would be worse off for one
more golden apple dropped to ground
without the least protesting sound,
and you would windfall lie, and we
forget your shimmer on the tree.

Beauty is always wasted: if
not Mignon's song sung to the deaf,
at all events to the unmoved.
A face like yours cannot be loved
long or seriously enough.
Almost, we seem to hold it off.

II

Well, you are tougher than I thought.
Now when the wash with ice hangs taut
this morning of St. Valentine,
I see you strip the squeaking line,
your body weighed against the load,
and all my groans can do no good.

Because you still are beautiful,
though squared and stiffened by the pull
of what nine windy years have done.
You have three daughters, lost a son.
I see all your intelligence
flung into that unwearied stance.

My envy is of no avail.
I turn my head and wish him well
who chafed your beauty into use
and lives forever in a house
lit by the friction of your mind.
You stagger in against the wind.

1958

THE ABSENT-MINDED
ARE ALWAYS TO BLAME

What do you look for down there
in the cracks of the pavement? Or up there
between the pineapple and the acanthus leaf
in that uninspired ornament? Odysseus
wading half-naked out of the shrubbery
like a god, dead serious among those at play,
could hardly be more out of it. In school
we striped your back with chalk, you all oblivious,
your eyes harnessed by a transparent strand
reaching the other side of things, or down
like a wellchain to the center of earth.
Now with those same eyes you pull the
pavements up like old linoleum,
arches of triumph start to liquefy
minutes after you slowly turn away.

1958

EURYCLEA'S TALE

I have to weep when I see it, the grown boy fretting
for a father dawdling among the isles,
and the seascape hollowed out by that boy's edged gaze
to receive one speck, one only, for years and years withheld.

And that speck, that curious man, has kept from home
till home would seem the forbidden place, till blood
and the tears of an old woman must run down
to satisfy the genius of place. Even then, what
can they do together, father and son?
the driftwood stranger and the rooted boy
whose eyes will have nothing then to ask the sea.

But all the time and everywhere
lies in ambush for the distracted eyeball
light: light on the ship racked up in port,
the chimney-stones, the scar whiter than smoke,
than her flanks, her hair, that true but aging bride.

1958

◈ SEPTEMBER 21

Wear the weight of equinoctial evening,
light like melons bruised on all the porches.
Feel the houses tenderly appraise you,
hold you in the watchfulness of mothers.

Once the nighttime was a milky river
washing past the swimmers in the sunset,
rinsing over sleepers of the morning.
Soon the night will be an eyeless quarry

where the shrunken daylight and its rebels,
loosened,   dive like stones in perfect silence,
names and voices drown without reflection.

Then the houses draw you. Then they have you.

1958

AFTER A SENTENCE
IN "MALTE LAURIDS BRIGGE"

The month's eye blurs.
The winter's lungs are cracked.
Along bloated gutters race,
shredded, your injured legions,
the waste of our remorseless search.
Your old, unuttered names are holes
worn in our skins
through which we feel from time to time
abrasive wind.

Those who are loved live poorly and in danger.
We who were loved will never
unlive that crippling fever.
A day returns, a certain weather
splatters the panes, and we
once more stare in the eye of our first failure.

1958

◈ SNAPSHOTS OF A
DAUGHTER-IN-LAW

1.

You, once a belle in Shreveport,
with henna-colored hair, skin like a peachbud,
still have your dresses copied from that time,
and play a Chopin prelude
called by Cortot: "*Delicious recollections
float like perfume through the memory.*"

Your mind now, mouldering like wedding-cake,
heavy with useless experience, rich
with suspicion, rumor, fantasy,
crumbling to pieces under the knife-edge
of mere fact. In the prime of your life.

Nervy, glowering, your daughter
wipes the teaspoons, grows another way.

2.

Banging the coffee-pot into the sink
she hears the angels chiding, and looks out
past the raked gardens to the sloppy sky.
Only a week since They said: *Have no patience.*

The next time it was: *Be insatiable.*
Then: *Save yourself; others you cannot save.*
Sometimes she's let the tapstream scald her arm,
a match burn to her thumbnail,

or held her hand above the kettle's snout
right in the woolly steam. They are probably angels,
since nothing hurts her any more, except
each morning's grit blowing into her eyes.

3.

A thinking woman sleeps with monsters.
The beak that grips her, she becomes. And Nature,
that sprung-lidded, still commodious
steamer-trunk of *tempora* and *mores*
gets stuffed with it all: the mildewed orange-flowers,
the female pills, the terrible breasts
of Boadicea beneath flat foxes' heads and orchids.

Two handsome women, gripped in argument,
each proud, acute, subtle, I hear scream
across the cut glass and majolica
like Furies cornered from their prey:
The argument *ad feminam*, all the old knives
that have rusted in my back, I drive in yours,
ma semblable, ma soeur!

4.

Knowing themselves too well in one another:
their gifts no pure fruition, but a thorn,
the prick filed sharp against a hint of scorn . . .
Reading while waiting
for the iron to heat,
writing, *My Life had stood—a Loaded Gun—*
in that Amherst pantry while the jellies boil and scum,
or, more often,
iron-eyed and beaked and purposed as a bird,
dusting everything on the whatnot every day of life.

5.

Dulce ridens, dulce loquens,
she shaves her legs until they gleam
like petrified mammoth-tusk.

6.

When to her lute Corinna sings
neither words nor music are her own;

only the long hair dipping
over her cheek, only the song
of silk against her knees
and these
adjusted in reflections of an eye.

Poised, trembling and unsatisfied, before
an unlocked door, that cage of cages,
tell us, you bird, you tragical machine—
is this *fertilisante douleur*? Pinned down
by love, for you the only natural action,
are you edged more keen
to prise the secrets of the vault? has Nature shown
her household books to you, daughter-in-law,
that her sons never saw?

7.

*"To have in this uncertain world some stay
which cannot be undermined, is
of the utmost consequence."*
                                    Thus wrote
a woman, partly brave and partly good,
who fought with what she partly understood.
Few men about her would or could do more,
hence she was labelled harpy, shrew and whore.

8.

"You all die at fifteen," said Diderot,
and turn part legend, part convention.
Still, eyes inaccurately dream
behind closed windows blankening with steam.
Deliciously, all that we might have been,
all that we were—fire, tears,
wit, taste, martyred ambition—
stirs like the memory of refused adultery
the drained and flagging bosom of our middle years.

9.

Not that it is done well, but
that it is done at all? Yes, think
of the odds! or shrug them off forever.
This luxury of the precocious child,
Time's precious chronic invalid,—
would we, darlings, resign it if we could?
Our blight has been our sinecure:
mere talent was enough for us—
glitter in fragments and rough drafts.

Sigh no more, ladies.
                              Time is male
and in his cups drinks to the fair.
Bemused by gallantry, we hear
our mediocrities over-praised,
indolence read as abnegation,
slattern thought styled intuition,
every lapse forgiven, our crime
only to cast too bold a shadow
or smash the mould straight off.

For that, solitary confinement,
tear gas, attrition shelling.
Few applicants for that honor.

10.   Well,

she's long about her coming, who must be
more merciless to herself than history.
Her mind full to the wind, I see her plunge
breasted and glancing through the currents,
taking the light upon her
at least as beautiful as any boy
or helicopter,
                    poised, still coming,
her fine blades making the air wince

but her cargo
no promise then:
delivered
palpable
ours.

1958–1960

PASSING ON

The landlord's hammer in the yard
patches a porch where your shirts swing
brashly against May's creamy blue.
This year the forsythia ran wild,
chrome splashed on the spring evenings,
every bush a pile of sulphur.
Now, ragged, they bend
under the late wind's onslaught, tousled
as my head beneath the clotheslines.

Soon we'll be off. I'll pack us into parcels,
stuff us in barrels, shroud us in newspapers,
pausing to marvel at old bargain sales:
Oh, all the chances we never seized!
Emptiness round the stoop of the house
minces, catwise, waiting for an in.

1959

THE RAVEN

If, antique hateful bird,
flapping through dawngagged streets
of metal shopfronts grated down
on pedestrian nerve-ends,

if, as on old film,
my features blurred and grained like cereal,
you find me walking up and down
waiting for my first dream,

don't try to sully my head
with vengeful squirtings. Fly on,
ratfooted cautionary of my dark,
till we meet further along.

You are no dream, old genius.
I smell you, get my teeth on edge,
stand in my sweat—in mercury—
even as you prime your feathers and set sail.

1959

◈ MERELY TO KNOW

I

Wedged in by earthworks
thrown up by snouters before me,
I kick and snuffle, breathing in
cobwebs of beetle-cuirass:
vainglory of polished green,
infallible pincer, resonant nerve,
a thickening on the air now,
confusion to my lungs, no more.
My predecessors blind me—
their zeal exhausted among roots and tunnels,
they gasped and looked up once or twice
into the beechtree's nightblack glitter.

II

Let me take you by the hair
and drag you backward to the light,
there spongelike press my gaze
patiently upon your eyes,
hold like a photographic plate
against you my enormous question.
What if you cringe, what if you weep?
Suffer this and you need suffer
nothing more. I'll give you back
yourself at last to the last part.
I take nothing, only look.
Change nothing. Have no need to change.
Merely to know and let you go.

1959

III

Spirit like water
moulded by unseen stone
and sandbar, pleats and funnels
according to its own
submerged necessity—
to the indolent eye
pure willfulness, to the stray
pine-needle boiling
in that cascade-bent pool
a random fury: Law,
if that's what's wanted, lies
asking to be read
in the dried brook-bed.

1961

ANTINOÜS: THE DIARIES

Autumn torture. The old signs
smeared on the pavement, sopping leaves
rubbed into the landscape as unguent on a bruise,
brought indoors, even, as they bring flowers, enormous,
with the colors of the body's secret parts.
All this. And then, evenings, needing to be out,
walking fast, fighting the fire
that must die, light that sets my teeth on edge with joy,
till on the black embankment
I'm a cart stopped in the ruts of time.

Then at some house the rumor of truth and beauty
saturates a room like lilac-water
in the steam of a bath, fires snap, heads are high,
gold hair at napes of necks, gold in glasses,
gold in the throat, poetry of furs and manners.
Why do I shiver then? Haven't I seen,
over and over, before the end of an evening,
the three opened coffins carried in and left in a corner?
Haven't I watched as somebody cracked his shin
on one of them, winced and hopped and limped
laughing to lay his hand on a beautiful arm
striated with hairs of gold, like an almond-shell?

The old, needless story. For if I'm here
it is by choice and when at last
I smell my own rising nausea, feel the air
tighten around my stomach like a surgical bandage,
I can't pretend surprise. What is it I so miscarry?
If what I spew on the tiles at last,
helpless, disgraced, alone,

is in part what I've swallowed from glasses, eyes,
motions of hands, opening and closing mouths,
isn't it also dead gobbets of myself,
abortive, murdered, or never willed?

1959

◈ JUVENILIA

Your Ibsen volumes, violet-spined,
each flaking its gold arabesque!
Again I sit, under duress, hands washed,
at your inkstained oaken desk,
by the goose-neck lamp in the tropic of your books,
stabbing the blotting-pad, doodling loop upon loop,
peering one-eyed in the dusty reflecting mirror
of your student microscope,
craning my neck to spell above me

A DOLLS HOUSE   LITTLE EYOLF
        WHEN WE DEAD AWAKEN

Unspeakable fairy tales ebb like blood through my head
as I dip the pen and for aunts, for admiring friends,
for you above all to read,
copy my praised and sedulous lines.

Behind the two of us, thirsty spines
quiver in semi-shadow, huge leaves uncurl and thicken.

1960

DOUBLE MONOLOGUE

To live illusionless, in the abandoned mine-
    shaft of doubt, and still
mime illusions for others? A puzzle
    for the maker who has thought
once too often too coldly.

Since I was more than a child
    trying on a thousand faces
I have wanted one thing: to know
    simply as I know my name
at any given moment, where I stand.

How much expense of time and skill
    which might have set itself
to angelic fabrications! All merely
    to chart one needle in the haymow?
Find yourself and you find the world?

Solemn presumption! Mighty Object
    no one but itself has missed,
what's lost, if you stay lost? Someone
    ignorantly loves you—will that serve?
Shrug that off, and presto!—

the needle drowns in the haydust.
    Think of the whole haystack—
a composition so fortuitous
    it only looks monumental.
There's always a straw twitching somewhere.

Wait out the long chance, and
    your needle too could get nudged up
to the apex of that bristling calm.

Rusted, possibly. You might not want
to swear it was the Object, after all.

Time wears us old utopians.
    I now no longer think
"truth" is the most beautiful of words.
    Today, when I see "truthful"
written somewhere, it flares

like a white orchid in wet woods,
    rare and grief-delighting, up from the page.
Sometimes, unwittingly even,
    we have been truthful.
In a random universe, what more

exact and starry consolation?
    Don't think I think
facts serve better than ignorant love.
    Both serve, and still
our need mocks our gear.

1960

A WOMAN MOURNED
BY DAUGHTERS

Now, not a tear begun,
we sit here in your kitchen,
spent, you see, already.
You are swollen till you strain
this house and the whole sky.
You, whom we so often
succeeded in ignoring!
You are puffed up in death
like a corpse pulled from the sea;
we groan beneath your weight.
And yet you were a leaf,
a straw blown on the bed,
you had long since become
crisp as a dead insect.
What is it, if not you,
that settles on us now
like satin you pulled down
over our bridal heads?
What rises in our throats
like food you prodded in?
Nothing could be enough.
You breathe upon us now
through solid assertions
of yourself: teaspoons, goblets,
seas of carpet, a forest
of old plants to be watered,
an old man in an adjoining
room to be touched and fed.
And all this universe
dares us to lay a finger
anywhere, save exactly
as you would wish it done.

1960

READINGS OF HISTORY

"He delighted in relating the fact that he had been born near Girgenti in a place called Chaos during a raging cholera epidemic."
—DOMENICO VITTORINI, *The Drama of Luigi Pirandello*

I: The Evil Eye

Last night we sat with the stereopticon,
laughing at genre views of 1906,
till suddenly, gazing straight into
that fringed and tasselled parlor, where the vestal
spurns an unlikely suitor
with hairy-crested plants to right and left,
my heart sank. It was terrible.
I smelled the mildew in those swags of plush,
dust on the eyepiece bloomed to freaks of mould.
I knew beyond all doubt how dead that couple was.

Today, a fresh clean morning.
Your camera stabs me unawares,
right in my mortal part.
A womb of celluloid already
contains my dotage and my total absence.

II: The Confrontation

Luigi Pirandello
looked like an old historian
(oval head, tufted white beard,
not least the hunger
for reconciliation in his eye).
For fourteen years, facing
his criminal reflection
in his wife's Grand Guignol mind,
he built over and over

that hall of mirrors
in which to be appears
to be perceived.

The present holds you like a raving wife,
clever as the mad are clever,
digging up your secret truths
from her disabled genius.
She knows what you hope
and dare not hope:
remembers
what you're sick
of forgetting.
What are you now
but what you know together, you and she?

She will not let you think.
It is important
to make connections. Everything
happens very fast in the minds
of the insane. Even you
aren't up to that, yet.
Go out, walk,
think of selves long past.

III: *Memorabilia*

I recall
Civil War letters of a great-grand-uncle,
fifteen at Chancellorsville,

                    no raconteur,
no speller, either; nor to put it squarely,
much of a mind;

               the most we gather
is that he did write home:

                    I am well,

how are my sisters, hope you are the same.
Did Spartan battle-echoes rack his head?
Dying, he turned into his father's memory.

History's queerly strong perfumes
rise from the crook of this day's elbow:
Seduction fantasies of the public mind,
or Dilthey's dream from which he roused to see
the cosmos glaring through his windowpane?
Prisoners of what we think occurred,
or dreamers dreaming toward a final word?

What, in fact, happened in these woods
on some obliterated afternoon?

IV: *Consanguinity*

Can history show us nothing
but pieces of ourselves, detached,
set to a kind of poetry,
a kind of music, even?
Seated today on Grandmamma's
plush sofa with the grapes
bursting so ripely from the curved mahogany,
we read the great Victorians
weeping, almost, as if
some family breach were healed.
Those angry giantesses and giants,
lately our kith and kin!
We stare into their faces, hear
at last what they were saying
(or some version not bruited
by filial irritation).

The cat-tails wither in the reading-room.
Tobacco-colored dust

drifts on the newest magazines.
I loaf here leafing ancient copies
of LIFE from World War II.
We look so poor and honest there:
girls with long hair badly combed
and unbecoming dresses—
where are you now?

                You sail
to shop in Europe, ignorantly freed
for you, an age ago.
Your nylon luggage matches

                              eyelids
expertly azured.
I, too, have lived in history.

V: *The Mirror*

Is it in hopes
to find or lose myself
that I
fill up my table now
with Michelet and Motley?
To "know how it was"
or to forget how it is—
what else?
Split at the root, neither Gentile nor Jew,
Yankee nor Rebel, born
in the face of two ancient cults,
I'm a good reader of histories.
And you,
Morris Cohen, dear to me as a brother,
when you sit at night
tracing your way through your volumes
of Josephus, or any
of the old Judaic chronicles,

do you find yourself there, a simpler,
more eloquent Jew?
or do you read
to shut out the tick-tock of self,
the questions and their routine answers?

VI: *The Covenant*

The present breaks our hearts. We lie and freeze,
our fingers icy as a bunch of keys.
Nothing will thaw these bones except
memory like an ancient blanket wrapped
about us when we sleep at home again,
smelling of picnics, closets, sicknesses,
old nightmare,
and insomnia's spreading stain.

Or say I sit with what I halfway know
as with a dying man who heaves the true
version at last, now that it hardly matters,
or gropes a hand to where the letters
sewn in the mattress can be plucked and read.
Here's water.   Sleep.   No more is asked of you.
I take your life into my living head.

1960

TO THE AIRPORT

Death's taxi crackles through the mist. The cheeks
 of diamond battlements flush high and cold.
Alarm clocks strike a million sparks of will.
Weeping: all night we've wept and watched the hours
that never will be ours again: Now
weeping, we roll through unforgettable
Zion, that rears its golden head from sleep
to act, and does not need us as we weep.

You dreamed us, City, and you let us be.
Grandiloquence, improvidence, ordure, light,
hours that seemed years, and ours—and over all
the endless wing of possibility,
that mackerel heaven of yours, fretted with all
our wits could leap for, envy batten on.
Our flights take off from you into the sea;
nothing you need wastes, though we think we do.

You are Canaan now and we are lifted high
to see all we were promised, never knew.

1960

THE AFTERWAKE

Nursing your nerves
to rest, I've roused my own; well,
now for a few bad hours!
Sleep sees you behind closed doors.
Alone, I slump in his front parlor.
You're safe inside. Good. But I'm
like a midwife who at dawn
has all in order: bloodstains
washed up, teapot on the stove,
and starts her five miles home
walking, the birthyell still
exploding in her head.

Yes, I'm with her now: here's
the streaked, livid road
edged with shut houses
breathing night out and in.
Legs tight with fatigue,
we move under morning's coal-blue star,
colossal as this load
of unexpired purpose, which drains
slowly, till scissors of cockcrow snip the air.

1961

ARTIFICIAL INTELLIGENCE
—to GPS—

Over the chessboard now,
Your Artificiality concludes
a final check; rests; broods—
      no—sorts and stacks a file of memories,
while I
concede the victory, bow,
and slouch among my free associations.

You never had a mother,
let's say? no digital Gertrude
whom you'd as lief have seen
Kingless? So your White Queen
was just an "operator."
(My Red had incandescence,
ire, aura, flare,
and trapped me several moments in her stare.)

I'm sulking, clearly, in the great tradition
of human waste. Why not
dump the whole reeking snarl
and let you solve me once for all?
(*Parameter*: a black-faced Luddite
itching for ecstasies of sabotage.)

Still, when
they make you write your poems, later on,
who'd envy you, force-fed
on all those variorum
editions of our primitive endeavors,

those frozen pemmican language-rations
they'll cram you with? denied
our luxury of nausea, you
forget nothing, have no dreams.

1961

A MARRIAGE IN THE 'SIXTIES

As solid-seeming as antiquity,
you frown above
the *New York Sunday Times*
where Castro, like a walk-on out of *Carmen*,
mutters into a bearded henchman's ear.

They say the second's getting shorter—
I knew it in my bones—
and pieces of the universe are missing.
I feel the gears of this late afternoon
slip, cog by cog, even as I read.
"I'm old," we both complain,
half-laughing, oftener now.

Time serves you well. That face—
part Roman emperor, part Raimu—
nothing this side of Absence can undo.
Bliss, revulsion, your rare angers can
only carry through what's well begun.

When
I read your letters long ago
in that half-defunct
hotel in Magdalen Street
every word primed my nerves.
A geographical misery
composed of oceans, fogbound planes
and misdelivered cablegrams
lay round me, a Nova Zembla
only your live breath could unfreeze.
Today we stalk
in the raging desert of our thought
whose single drop of mercy is

each knows the other there.
Two strangers, thrust for life upon a rock,
may have at last the perfect hour of talk
that language aches for; still—
two minds, two messages.

Your brows knit into flourishes. Some piece
of mere time has you tangled there.
Some mote of history has flown into your eye.
Will nothing ever be the same,
even our quarrels take a different key,
our dreams exhume new metaphors?
The world breathes underneath our bed.
Don't look. We're at each other's mercy too.

Dear fellow-particle, electric dust
I'm blown with—ancestor
to what euphoric cluster—
see how particularity dissolves
in all that hints of chaos. Let one finger
hover toward you from There
and see this furious grain
suspend its dance to hang
beside you like your twin.

1961

FIRST THINGS

I can't name love now
without naming its object—
this the final measure
of those flintspark years
when one believed
one's flash innate.
Today I swear
only in the sun's eye
do I take fire.

1961

◈ ATTENTION

The ice age is here.
I sit burning cigarettes,
burning my brain.
A micro-Tibet,
deadly, frivolous, complete,
blinds the four panes.
Veils of dumb air
unwind like bandages
from my lips
half-parted, steady as the mouths
of antique statues.

1961

END OF AN ERA

This morning, flakes of sun
peel down to the last snowholds,
the barbed-wire leavings of a war
lost, won, in these dead-end alleys.
Stale as a written-out journalist,
I sort my gear.—Nothing is happening.—City,
dumb as a pack of thumbed cards, you
once had snap and glare
and secret life; now, trembling
under my five grey senses' weight,
you flatten
onto the table.

Baudelaire, I think of you . . . Nothing changes,
rude and self-absorbed the current
dashes past, reflecting nothing, poetry
extends its unsought amnesty,
the roots of the great grove
atrophy underground.
Some voices, though, shake in the air like heat.

The neighborhood is changing,
even the neighbors are grown, methinks, peculiar.
I walk into my house and see
tourists fingering this and that.
My mirrors, my bric-à-brac
don't suit their style.

Those old friends, though,
alive and dead,
for whom things don't come easy—
Certain forests are sawdust,
from now on have to be described?
Nothing changes.   The bones of the mammoths
are still in the earth.

1961

RUSTICATION

In a gigantic *pot de chambre*, scrolled
with roses, purchased dearly at auction,
goldenrod and asters spill
toward the inevitable sunset.
The houseguests trail from swimming
under huge towels.
Marianne dangles barefoot in the hammock
reading about Martin Luther King.
Vivaldi rattles on the phonograph,
flutes ricocheting off the birchtrees.
Flies buzz and are gaily murdered.

Still out of it, and guilty,
I glue the distance-glasses to my eyes
ostrich-like, hoping
you'll think me in that clearing half a mile away.
Offstage I hear
the old time-killers dressing, banging doors,
your voice, a timbre or two too rich for love,
cheering them on.
A kestrel sails into my field of vision,
clear as a rising star.

Why should I need to quarrel
with another's consolations?
Why, in your mortal skin,
vigorously smashing ice and smoking,
a graying pigtail down your back,
should you seem infamous to me?

1961

◈ APOLOGY

I've said: I wouldn't ever
keep a cat, a dog,
a bird—
chiefly because
I'd rather love my equals.
Today, turning
in the fog of my mind,
I knew, the thing I really
couldn't stand in the house
is a woman
with a mindful of fog
and bloodletting claws
and the nerves of a bird
and the nightmares of a dog.

1961

◈ SISTERS

Can I easily say,
I know you of course now,
no longer the fellow-victim,
reader of my diaries, heir
to my outgrown dresses,
ear for my poems and invectives?
Do I know you better
than that blue-eyed stranger
self-absorbed as myself
raptly knittting or sleeping
through a thirdclass winter journey?
Face to face all night
her dreams and whimpers
tangled with mine,
sleeping but not asleep
behind the engine drilling
into dark Germany,
her eyes, mouth, head
reconstructed by dawn
as we nodded farewell.
Her I should recognize
years later, anywhere.

1961

IN THE NORTH

Mulish, unregenerate,
   not "as all men are"
   but more than most

you sit up there in the sunset;
   there are only three
   hours of dark

in your night. You are
   alone as an old king
   with his white-gold beard

when in summer the ships
   sail out, the heroes
   singing, push off

for other lands. Only
   in winter when
   trapped in the ice

your kingdom flashes
   under the northern lights
   and the bees dream

in their hives, the young
   men like the bees
   hang near you

for lack of another,
   remembering too, with some
   remorseful tenderness

you are their king.

1962

PEELING ONIONS

Only to have a grief
equal to all these tears!

There's not a sob in my chest.
Dry-hearted as Peer Gynt
I pare away, no hero,
merely a cook.

Crying was labor, once
when I'd good cause.
Walking, I felt my eyes like wounds
raw in my head,
so postal-clerks, I thought, must stare.
A dog's look, a cat's, burnt to my brain—
yet all that stayed
stuffed in my lungs like smog.

These old tears in the chopping-bowl.

1961

GHOST OF A CHANCE

You see a man
trying to think.

You want to say
to everything:
Keep off! Give him room!
But you only watch,
terrified
the old consolations
will get him at last
like a fish
half-dead from flopping
and almost crawling
across the shingle,
almost breathing
the raw, agonizing
air
till a wave
pulls it back blind into the triumphant
sea.

1962

THE WELL

Down this old well
what leaves have fallen,
what cores of eaten apples,
what scraps of paper!
An old trash barrel.
November, no one comes.

But I come, trying
to breathe that word
into the well's ear
which could make the leaves fly up
like a green jet
to clothe the naked tree,
the whole fruit leap to the bough,
the scraps like fleets of letters
sail up into my hands.

Leiden, 1961

◈ NOVELLA

Two people in a room, speaking harshly.
One gets up, goes out to walk.
(That is the man.)
The other goes into the next room
and washes the dishes, cracking one.
(That is the woman.)
It gets dark outside.
The children quarrel in the attic.
She has no blood left in her heart.
The man comes back to a dark house.
The only light is in the attic.
He has forgotten his key.
He rings at his own door
and hears sobbing on the stairs.
The lights go on in the house.
The door closes behind him.
Outside, separate as minds,
the stars too come alight.

1962

FACE

I could look at you a long time,
man of red and blue;
your eye glows mockingly
from the rainbow-colored flesh
Karel Appel clothed you in.
You are a fish,
drawn up dripping hugely
from the sea of paint,
laid on the canvas
to glower and flash
out of the blackness
that is your true element.

1962

PROSPECTIVE IMMIGRANTS
PLEASE NOTE

Either you will
go through this door
or you will not go through.

If you go through
there is always the risk
of remembering your name.

Things look at you doubly
and you must look back
and let them happen.

If you do not go through
it is possible
to live worthily

to maintain your attitudes
to hold your position
to die bravely

but much will blind you,
much will evade you,
at what cost who knows?

The door itself
makes no promises.
It is only a door.

1962

◈ LIKENESS

A good man
   is an odd thing:
   hard to find
as the song says,

he is anarchic
   as a mountain freshet
   and unprotected
by the protectors.

1962

◈ ALWAYS THE SAME

Slowly, Prometheus
bleeds to life
in his huge loneliness.

You, for whom
his bowels are exposed,
go about your affairs

dying a little every day
from the inside out
almost imperceptibly

till the late decades when
women go hysterical
and men are dumbly frightened

and far away, like the sea
Prometheus sings on
"like a battle-song after a battle."

1962

PEACE

Lashes of white light
binding another hailcloud—
the whole onset all over
bursting against our faces,
sputtering like dead holly
fired in a grate:
And the birds go mad
potted by grapeshot
while the sun shines
in one quarter of heaven
and the rainbow
breaks out its enormous flag—
oily, unnegotiable—
over the sack-draped backs
of the cattle in their kingdom.

1961

THE ROOFWALKER

for Denise

Over the half-finished houses
night comes. The builders
stand on the roof. It is
quiet after the hammers,
the pulleys hang slack.
Giants, the roofwalkers,
on a listing deck, the wave
of darkness about to break
on their heads. The sky
is a torn sail where figures
pass magnified, shadows
on a burning deck.

I feel like them up there:
exposed, larger than life,
and due to break my neck.

Was it worth while to lay—
with infinite exertion—
a roof I can't live under?
—All those blueprints,
closings of gaps,
measurings, calculations?
A life I didn't choose
chose me: even
my tools are the wrong ones
for what I have to do.
I'm naked, ignorant,
a naked man fleeing
across the roofs
who could with a shade of difference
be sitting in the lamplight
against the cream wallpaper
reading—not with indifference—
about a naked man
fleeing across the roofs.

1961

◈ NOTES ON THE POEMS

"SNAPSHOTS OF A DAUGHTER-IN-LAW"

4. "My Life had stood—a Loaded Gun," Emily Dickinson, *Complete Poems,* ed. T. H. Johnson, 1960, p. 369.
7. ". . . is of the utmost consequence," from Mary Wollstonecraft, *Thoughts on the Education of Daughters,* London, 1787.
8. "Vous mourez toutes à quinze ans," from the *Lettres à Sophie Volland,* quoted by Simone de Beauvoir in *Le Deuxième Sexe,* vol. II, pp. 123–4.
10. Cf. *Le Deuxième Sexe,* vol. II, p. 574: ". . . elle arrive du fond des ages, de Thèbes, de Minos, de Chichen Itza; et elle est aussi le totem planté au coeur de la brousse africaine; c'est un hélicoptère et c'est un oiseau; et voilà la plus grande merveille: sous ses cheveux peints le bruissement des feuillages devient une pensée et des paroles s'échappent de ses seins."

"ARTIFICIAL INTELLIGENCE"

See Herbert Simon, *The New Science of Management Decision,* p. 26. "*A General Problem-Solving Program:* Computer programs have been written that enable computers to discover proofs for theorems in logic or geometry, to play chess, to design motors . . . to compose music . . . From almost all of them, whether intended as simulations [of human processes] or not, we learn something about human problem solving, thinking, and learning.

"The first thing we learn . . . is that we can explain these human processes *without* postulating mechanisms at subconscious levels that are different from those that are partly conscious and partly verbalized. . . . The secret of problem solving is that there is no secret."

"ALWAYS THE SAME"

The last line is quoted from D. H. Lawrence, letter to Henry Savage, in *The Collected Letters of D. H. Lawrence,* ed. Harry T. Moore, vol. I, p. 258.